Basic Tips and Instructions for Sea

Nature's Treasures from the Sea!
Follow our Never-Fail instructions to create angels, home decor items, jewelry and exquisite gifts using beautiful seashells from the ocean's doorstep. Just choose your favorite shells, arrange and glue in place. Add assorted trims and spray with sealer for beautiful finished pieces.

Basic Materials:

Seashells
GOOP or E6000 glue
Wax paper
Hot glue pad

Hot glue and glue gun
DecoArt paint
Assorted trims

Working with Seashells

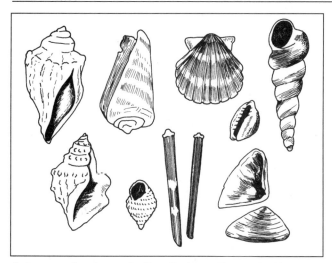

Select unbroken shells. Only collect shells that have been washed up on the beach. Shells still in the water may contain a living animal.

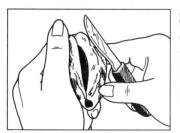

Scrape away barnacles and lime build up with a small sharp knife or old dental pick.

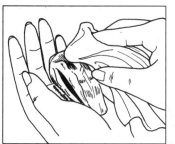

Wipe away surface sand and dirt with a damp cloth, rubbing hard on stubborn spots.

Whiten discolored sanddollars and shells by soaking in a solution of one part chlorine bleach to four parts water.

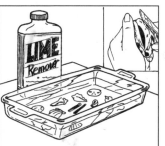

Remove stubborn-buildup by soaking then scraping. Some shells require up to a month of soaking and scraping but can be cleaned with patience and a lot of elbow grease. Lime remover bathroom tile cleaners are also useful for cleaning shells.

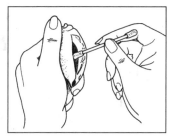

To clean openings in small shells, pry out sand and dirt with a nut pick and wipe clean with a cotton swab.

Dry wet shells thoroughly, up to several hours for soaked shells. Glue will not stick to wet or damp shells.

Continued

Clean broken shells and fragments and display in glass jars and small baskets.

Glue Shells

Protect work surface with newspapers, wax paper or hot glue pad.

Position each shell before gluing. Glue shells on objects to be decorated with E6000, GOOP or hot glue.

Glue shells to each other with hot glue for freestanding shell projects. Do not stir or spread glue with nozzle since mixing weakens the bonding power. Shells remain hot for a long period of time after gluing. Use caution when touching shells after gluing.

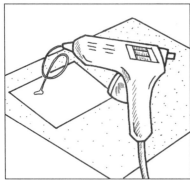

To prevent glue strings, lift nozzle of gun 12" from surface and twirl around glue string. The heat of the nozzle will melt strings before they harden.

Mix 1 part White glue with 2 parts water and paint over surface of sanddollars to strengthen the fragile shell.

Spray finished projects with a Clear gloss acrylic sealer. Satin or matte finish sealers may also be used, but a gloss will make your shells look as if they've just been kissed by the sea.

There are many beautiful shells available. The shells used in each project have been listed but other shells may be substituted. Be creative!

Tip: Prevent Hot Glue Burns

If hot glue drips on your skin or sticks to your fingers, quickly bite off glue with your teeth and spit it out. It may seem unsanitary but the glue has been sterilized by the heat and is not toxic or water soluble. Your teeth and mouth are wet and cold so glue will not stick to them. **Do not attempt to pick off glue with lips or dry fingers, glue is hot enough to cause burns.**

For glue drips on clothing, hold fabric away from skin until glue cools. **Do not attempt to remove or wipe off while hot**, the glue will become embedded in the fabric fibers. Place a cold wet cloth or an ice cube behind glue for a few minutes and pick off glue. Dry clean to remove remaining glue.

SHELLS:
2 Bursa Crumena (roof, flowerpot)
13 Dyed Dove (star, flowers)

60 White Chula (roof)	8 Mexican Olive (hole)
28 Baby Ark (roof edge)	6 Turitella (star)
1 Small Snail (perch)	1 Coquina (hole)
1 Small Babylonia (flower pot)	2 Trochus (star, sign)
1 Cancellaria Undulat (body)	2 Baby Ark (wings)
1 Snail (head)	1 Tiny Auger (beak)

INSTRUCTIONS:
Birdhouse - Spray paint Off White, let dry. Spray with Stone Craft paint. Cut 8 pieces of rope the same length as roof. Glue 4 pieces on each side along edges of ridges and at top. Glue chula shells to roof. Glue baby arks along edges of roof.

Posts - Cut twig into 8 pieces, glue to edge around base for posts. Starting at front glue one end of jute to top of post, wrap around each post ending at post on opposite side of front. Cut and glue pieces of rope between posts around base.

Sign - Write 'SEAVIEW INN' on wood rectangle, glue to front. Glue jute around edge and trochus to top of sign.

Hole - Referring to photo, glue Mexican olive shells around hole in front with coquina at base.

Perch - Wrap jute around perch, glue in place. Glue small snail shell to end.

Flower Pot - Glue one Bursa Crumena to front of house at base with opening facing up. Cut 3" of sisal rope. Glue one end inside opening of flower pot. Feather strands of rope. Add small pieces of baby's breath and glue dove shells to some rope strands.

Finish - Glue remaining Bursa Crumena to top front of house. Bird - Referring to photo for placement, glue beak to head, head to body and wings to sides of body. Glue toothpicks inside shell for legs, perch on top of house.

Back of Birdhouse - Glue trochus to center and turitella around snail shells. Glue small dove shells in spaces between turitella.

Seaview Inn Birdhouse
FRONT COVER PHOTO
MATERIALS:
Walnut Hollow chalet bird house
Off White spray paint
Krylon Stone Craft spray paint
1" x 1¼" wood rectangle
Sisal rope
Jute twine
16" x ½" sturdy twig
Dried baby's breath
2 toothpicks
Black fine-tip permanent pen

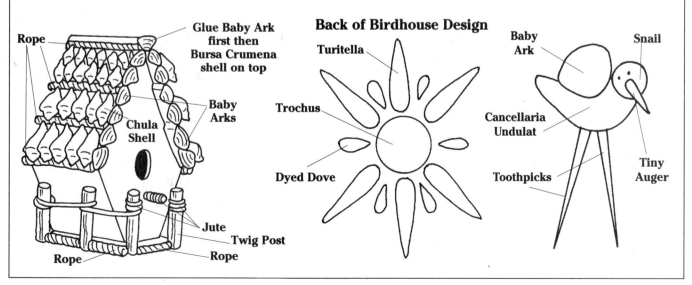

Back of Birdhouse Design

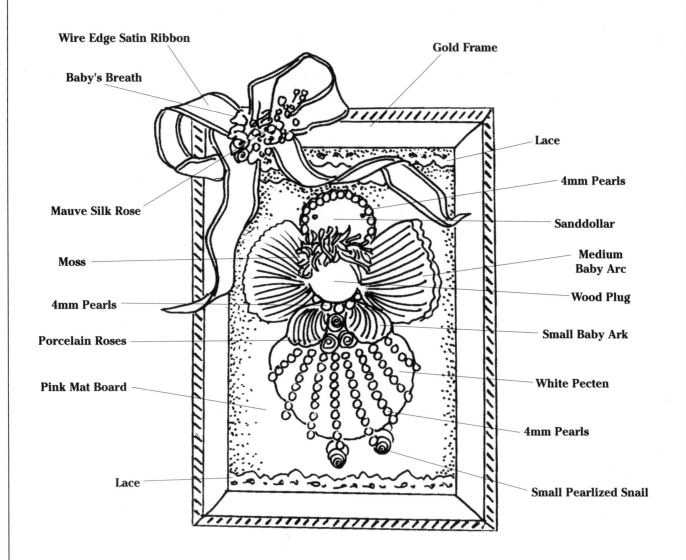

Wire Edge Satin Ribbon

Baby's Breath

Mauve Silk Rose

Moss

4mm Pearls

Porcelain Roses

Pink Mat Board

Lace

Gold Frame

Lace

4mm Pearls

Sanddollar

Medium Baby Arc

Wood Plug

Small Baby Ark

White Pecten

4mm Pearls

Small Pearlized Snail

Angel Picture
FRONT COVER PHOTO

MATERIALS:
Gold frame with 4" x 6" opening
4" x 6" of Pink mat board
18" of ⅝" Off White/Gold wire edge satin ribbon
Dried baby's breath
Mauve silk rose
9" of ½" Off White ruffled lace
18" Off White 4mm pearls on a string
Gold ring
¾" wood button plug
Sphagnum moss
3 Pink ¼" porcelain roses

SHELLS:
1 Small Sanddollar (halo)
2 Medium Baby Arks (wings)
2 Small Baby Arks (arms)   1 White Pecten (dress)
2 Small Pearlized Snail (feet)

INSTRUCTIONS:
Remove glass from frame. Glue lace to inside bottom and top edges of frame. Glue mat in opening. Referring to photo, glue shells for dress, wings and halo in place. Glue wood plug in center for head. Glue moss on head and shells for arms on front of dress. Glue pearls along indentations in dress shell, around neck and around top edge of sanddollar. Glue porcelain roses on front of dress and ring on head. Glue on feet. Tie ribbon bow, glue in place. Glue small sprigs of baby's breath and silk rose to center of bow.

Sailor's Love Knot

FRONT COVER PHOTO

MATERIALS:

28" of sisal rope

36" of ½" Seafoam Green satin ribbon

36" of White 4mm pearls on a string

Small Mauve silk rose

Sprigs of dried baby's breath

SHELLS:

6 Baby Ark   6 Turitella

INSTRUCTIONS:

Fold rope in shape of heart as shown in photo, secure with glue. Wrap ribbon around rope, glue ends. Wrap pearls around rope on top of ribbon, glue. Fray ends of rope and separate strands. Glue shells where rope joins. Glue rose to center of shells and baby's breath around rose.

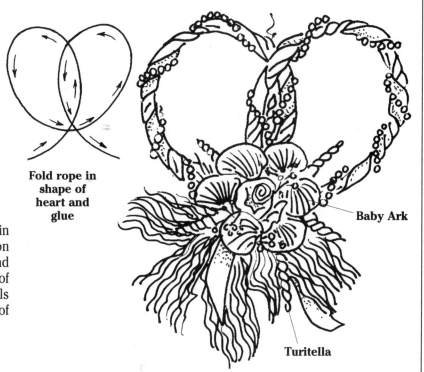

Fold rope in
shape of
heart and
glue

Baby Ark

Turitella

Hair Barrette

FRONT COVER PHOTO

MATERIALS

3" metal barrette

3" plastic oval base

9" of ½" Off White gathered lace

SHELLS:

Small and Medium Dyed Pearlized Craft

3 Pearlized Turbo   2 Babylonia

INSTRUCTIONS:

Glue barrette to plastic base with E6000. Glue lace around edge of base. Arrange and glue shells on base with larger shells in center.

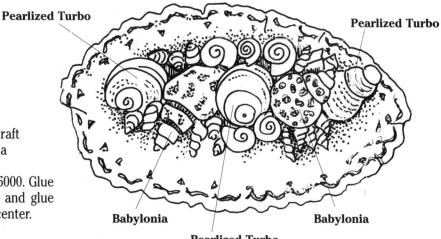

Pearlized Turbo

Pearlized Turbo

Babylonia

Babylonia

Pearlized Turbo

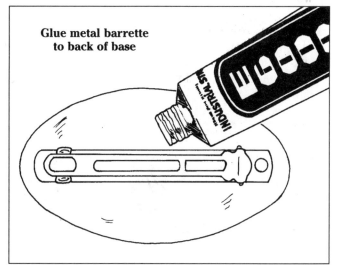

Glue metal barrette
to back of base

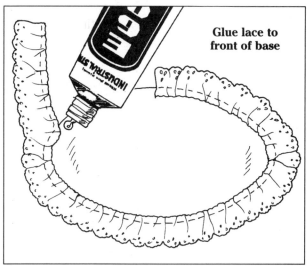

Glue lace to
front of base

Shell Vendor Doll

FRONT COVER PHOTO

MATERIALS:
1" wood ball knob
9" of ¼" Pink satin ribbon
4mm x 9mm teardrop pearl charm
Beige curly wool hair
1½" oval basket
Pink cosmetic blush
Black fine-tip permanent pen
Small Brass heart charm

SHELLS:

3 Baking Dish (dress)   1 White Pecten (hat)
1 Pink Pecten (apron)   2 Turitella (arms)
5 Assorted Small Shells (basket)

INSTRUCTIONS:

Overlap and glue two baking dish shells at top. Place and glue third shell over the top of the first two shells for skirt. Glue ball knob to top. Rub blush on face. Dot eyes with pen. Glue hair on head. Glue pecten to back of head for hat. Glue Pink pecten to front of dress for apron and turitella to each side for arms. Make ribbon bow, secure with wire. Attach pearl to wire. Glue bow to front of apron. Glue small shells in basket and heart charm on front of basket. Glue basket to dress and end of arm.

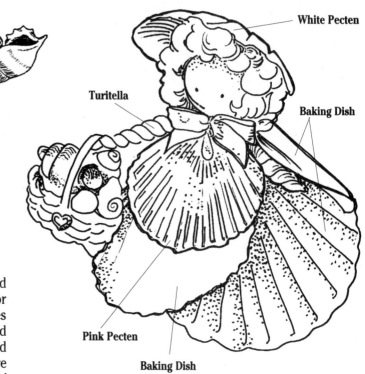

White Pecten

Turitella

Baking Dish

Pink Pecten

Baking Dish

Doll Assembly

Glue Baking Dish Shells in order shown

A 1

B 2 1

C 2 4 3 1

D Wood Ball

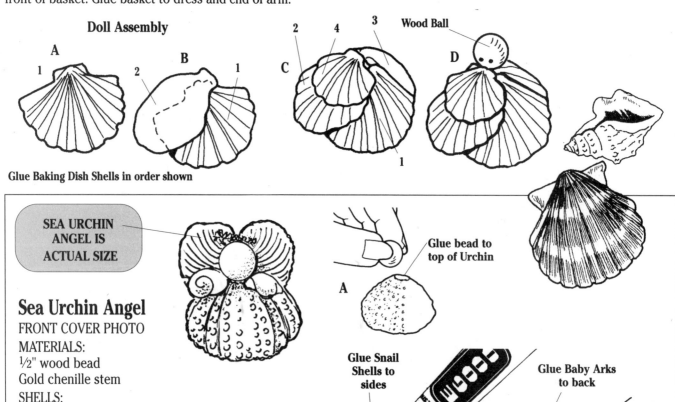

SEA URCHIN ANGEL IS ACTUAL SIZE

Sea Urchin Angel

FRONT COVER PHOTO

MATERIALS:
½" wood bead
Gold chenille stem

SHELLS:

1 Small Pink Urchin   2 Baby Ark (wings)
2 Snail (arms)

INSTRUCTIONS:

Glue bead to top of urchin, snail shells to sides and baby arks to back. Curl chenille stem around pencil to shape halo. Glue to back of head.

A Glue bead to top of Urchin

B Glue Snail Shells to sides

C

D Glue Baby Arks to back

Curl chenille stem around pencil

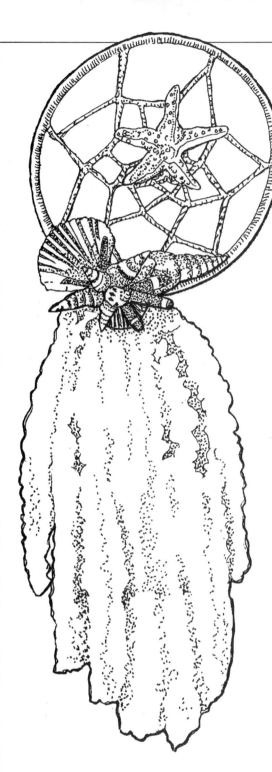

DreamCatcher

CENTER PHOTO

MATERIALS:
9" embroidery hoop
Jute string
Off White curly crepe wool hair

SHELLS:

2 Black Scallop	1 Tibia Curta
4 Turris	1 Babylonia
1 Starfish	5 Sea Urchin Spine

INSTRUCTIONS:
Cover hoop by wrapping with jute. Tie a web with 7 points and 5 rows. Cut curly hair into 3 equal pieces. Fold in half. Tie small piece of string around fold, tie to hoop. Pull wool strands gently apart to fluff. Glue shells to hoop and starfish to center of web. Display on wall or hang in window.

DreamCatcher Web

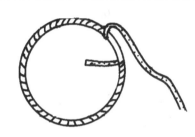

Wrap Hoop. Glue one end of string on hoop leaving a 6" tail. Wrap hoop to starting point, leave 6" tail. Secure the end with glue. Tie tails together for hanger.

Make Web. Tie one end of string on hoop. Keeping string pulled snug, tie half hitches at evenly spaced intervals forming loops.

Make Space between the last half hitch and the starting point smaller than the other spaces to keep gap from forming. Tie the next half-hitch in the center of the first loop. Continue tying required number of rows. Tie off in a knot.

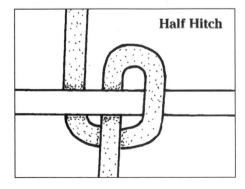

Half Hitch

Wreath
CENTER PHOTO
MATERIALS USED:
10" bleached vine wreath
Green Eucalyptus
SHELLS:
2 White Scallop
7 Assorted Slices   3 Babylonia
1 Small Pink Urchin   1 King's Crown
INSTRUCTIONS:
Glue scallops to wreath at 4" intervals. Referring to photo, glue larger shells between scallops. Add shell slices, eucalyptus and urchin shell.

1" mini wood bucket
Small piece of floral foam
Gloss varnish
Wax paper
Glue gun
SHELLS:
Assortment of Apple Blossom and Coquina Shells (petals)
Dentalium (butterfly)   Small Snail Shell
INSTRUCTIONS:
Frame and Mat - Place mat board in frame opening. Glue ribbon around mat for border, (see pattern for placement). Glue pearls on inside edge of frame.

Basket - Glue base of bucket to center of doily. Fold edges of doily up around bucket, glue in place on front and back. Tightly pack bucket with floral foam. Tie bow with remaining ribbon, glue on front of doily.

Pansies - Make two. Place 2 coquina and 1 apple blossom face down on wax paper, glue together. Let dry, turn shells over. Place small dab of glue where shells join, place 2 smaller coquina shells in glue. Let dry. Glue small pearl to center.

Roses - Make two large and one small. Place a dab of glue on wax paper. Working quickly, gently press 5 apple blossom shells in glue at a slight angle. Let dry. Place more glue in center and press 4 more shells in glue. Let dry, gently remove from wax paper. Glue pearl in center. Make small rose with 3 outer and 3 inner shells, glue pearl in center.

Shell Flowers Frame
CENTER PHOTO
MATERIALS:
Wood frame with 5" x 7" opening
5" x 7" of Green mat board
24" of Off White 4mm pearls on string
Green floral wire
3" round White crocheted doily
1 yard of 1/8" White/Gold ribbon
2 Red seed beads

Actual Size Placement Pattern

Flower Assembly

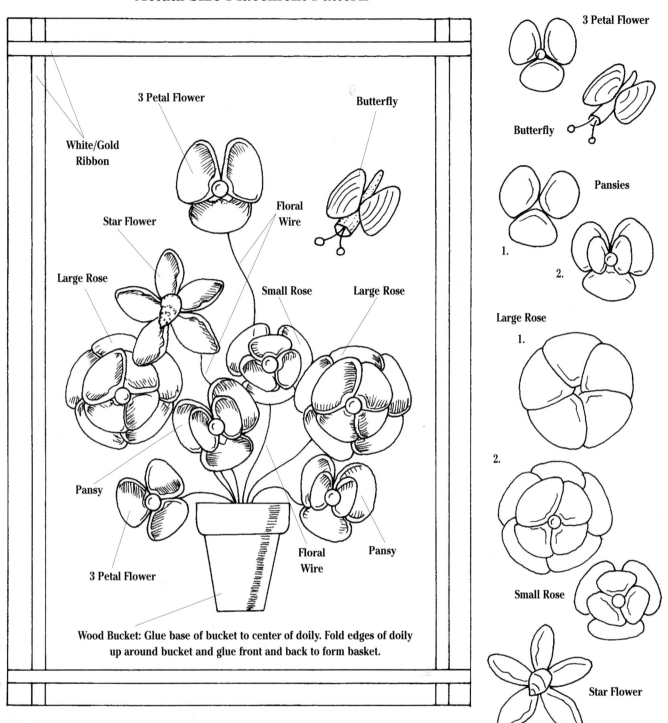

3 Petal Flower

Butterfly

White/Gold Ribbon

3 Petal Flower

Butterfly

Star Flower

Floral Wire

Pansies

1.

2.

Large Rose

Small Rose

Large Rose

Large Rose

1.

2.

Pansy

Floral Wire

Pansy

3 Petal Flower

Small Rose

Star Flower

Wood Bucket: Glue base of bucket to center of doily. Fold edges of doily up around bucket and glue front and back to form basket.

Star Flower - Make one. Place 5 coquina shells face down on wax paper, glue in center. Let dry, remove from wax paper. Glue small snail shell in center.

3-Petal Flower - Make two. Place 3 coquina shells face down on wax paper, glue in center. Let dry, remove from wax paper. Glue pearl in center.

Finish Flowers - When all flowers have been completed, glue 4" of floral wire to back of each. Spray with gloss var-

nish. Arrange in vase by gluing wire stems into floral foam. Larger roses should also be glued on mat to support weight.

Butterfly - Glue 2 small coquina shells to dentalium. Cut 1" of wire and bend in half, glue seed bead to each end. Glue wire inside open end of dentalium. Glue butterfly on mat.

Hexagon Box

CENTER PHOTO

MATERIALS:

8" hexagon papier maché box
6" round Ecru crocheted doily
3" Ecru tassel
24" of ¼" Ecru satin ribbon
24" of 1⅞" Ecru lace
Buttermilk and Mink Tan DecoArt paint
Sponge brush
Small sponge

SHELLS:

1 Orange Pecten	3 Philippine Olive
1 Baby Ark	2 Turris
1 Babylonia	1 Rose Cockle
3 Venus Clam	2 Yellow Banded Snail
1 Bursa Crumena	

INSTRUCTIONS:

Paint box with 2 coats of Buttermilk using sponge brush. When dry, dampen sponge in water, dip in Mink Tan, blot on paper towel and apply over Buttermilk. Let dry. Spray box with sealer.

Glue doily to center of lid. Glue lace around bottom of box with lower edge level with bottom of box. Glue ribbon around top edge of lace. Glue tassel under edge and shells on top of doily.

Glue doily to center of lid. Glue lace around bottom of box.

Mirror

CENTER PHOTO

MATERIALS:

7" round wood plaque with routed edge
4" round mirror
Sawtooth picture hanger
2 yards of White pearls on a string
Natural raffia
Off White spray paint

SHELLS:

1 Pink Pecten	6 Rose Cockle
1 Pink Murex	6 Coquina
1 Turris	2 Pearlized Turbo
2 Babylonia	3 Venus Clam
6 Mexican Olive	15 Coral Pieces

INSTRUCTIONS:

Spray paint wood plaque. When dry, attach hanger to back near upper edge. Glue mirror to center front. Tightly twist lengths of raffia together to form a ½" diameter rope. Wrap pearls around rope. Glue rope to outside edge of plaque. Starting with larger shells, arrange shells on plaque around edge of mirror, glue large shells in place. Fill spaces with small shells.

NOTE: If you wish to spray the shells with a varnish, this must be done before gluing to plaque.

Driftwood Birds

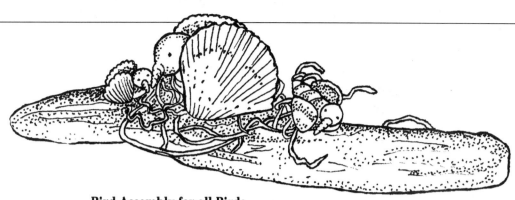

CENTER PHOTO

MATERIALS:

Driftwood or other
  decorative wood piece
Black fine-tip permanent
  pen
Excelsior

SHELLS:

1 Medium and 2 Small
  Strombus Canarium (bodies)
1 Medium and 2 Small Cats' Eyes (heads)
2 Baby Ark (wings)
2 Cockle (wings)
2 White Scallop (wings)
3 Small Turitella (beak)

INSTRUCTIONS:

Referring to photo for placement, glue beaks to head, head to body and wings to sides of body. Glue birds to driftwood. Glue excelsior around base of birds.

Bird Assembly for all Birds

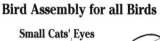
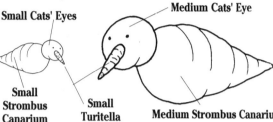
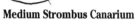
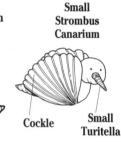

Small Cats' Eyes — Medium Cats' Eye — Small Cats' Eyes

Small Strombus Canarium — Small Turitella — Medium Strombus Canarium — Small Strombus Canarium

Small Baby Ark — Scallop — Cockle — Small Turitella

Shell Clock

CENTER PHOTO

SHELLS:

Walnut Hollow 5" x 7" wood clock
Quartz clock movement with a $^{15}/_{16}$" shaft
2" Gold serpentine clock hands
DecoArt paint (Ice Blue acrylic, Dazzling Metallics
  Ice Blue, Sparkling Sandstone Light Blue)
Paintbrush
Krylon spray satin finish

SHELLS:

1 Yellow Banded Snail	2 Starfish
2 Cowrie	4 Coral Pieces
1 Tibia Curta	Assorted Natural Small Craft
1 Philippine Olive	

INSTRUCTIONS:

Paint clock Ice Blue. Paint over base and edges on side and top with Ice Blue dazzling metallic acrylic. Paint over front of clock with Light Blue sparkling sandstone. Let dry. Glue small craft shells on front of clock for numbers, using larger shells for the numbers 3, 6, 9 and 12. Glue one small shell to end of second hand. Glue coral pieces to bottom left of clock. Glue remaining shells referring to photo. Glue tibia curta shell to top of clock. Spray with sealer. Insert clock and attach hands following manufacturer's instructions.

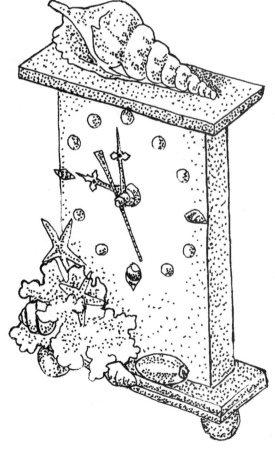

Shell Doll on Ribbon

CENTER PHOTO

MATERIALS:

¾" wood ball

Jute twine

⅛" diameter knitting needle or dowel

18" of ⅛" Blue ribbon

4" of White 3mm strung pearls

SHELLS:

2 White Scallop (same size)   1 Small Snail

1 Tiny Trochus   1 Trochus

INSTRUCTIONS:

Glue scallops together back to back. Glue bead to top.

Hair - Wrap jute around a knitting needle. Hold in place and lay a thin bead of hot glue along jute. When glue is dry, remove jute from needle. Glue trochus to top of head and hair around edge of shell. Glue pearls around top of hair.

Necklace - Glue remaining pearls around neck and tiny trochus to center front.

Hanger - Thread 8" of ribbon through space between scallop shells, tie ends together for hanger. Make bow with remaining ribbon, glue to top of hanger. Glue snail shell to center of bow.

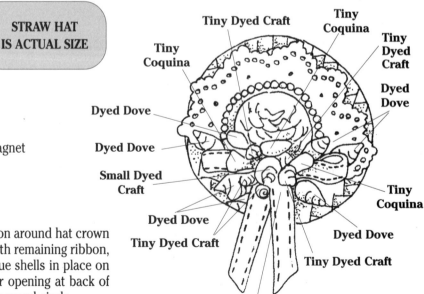

Small Snail

Tiny Trochus

Scallops

To Make Hair:

A. Wrap jute around knitting needle

B. Lay a thin bead of hot glue along jute

C. Remove jute from needle

Back View of Hair

E. Glue Hair

D. Glue Trochus

F. Glue Pearls

Straw Hat

CENTER PHOTO

MATERIALS:

2" straw hat

4" of ½" Off White ruffled lace

12" of ¼" Off White satin ribbon

4" of White 3mm strung pearls

1" wood circle

Pin back, button cover or ½" round magnet

SHELLS:

5 Tiny and 1 Small Dyed Craft

4 Tiny Coquina   7 Dyed Dove

INSTRUCTIONS:

Glue lace around brim of hat. Glue ribbon around hat crown and pearls on top of ribbon. Tie bow with remaining ribbon, glue to hat brim. Referring to photo, glue shells in place on and around bow. Glue wood circle over opening at back of hat. Glue pin, magnet or button cover to wood circle.

STRAW HAT IS ACTUAL SIZE

Tiny Dyed Craft

Tiny Coquina

Tiny Dyed Craft

Tiny Coquina

Dyed Dove

Dyed Dove

Dyed Dove

Small Dyed Craft

Tiny Coquina

Dyed Dove

Dyed Dove

Tiny Dyed Craft

Tiny Dyed Craft

Tiny Coquina

Sea Grass Basket

CENTER PHOTO

MATERIALS:
6" oval sea grass basket
4" Ecru crocheted doily

SHELLS:
5 Assorted Slices
3 Babylonia
7 Cowrie
1 Medium Baby Ark
1 Trochus

INSTRUCTIONS:
Glue doily to basket lid. Arrange shells. Glue larger shells in place. Add smaller shells.

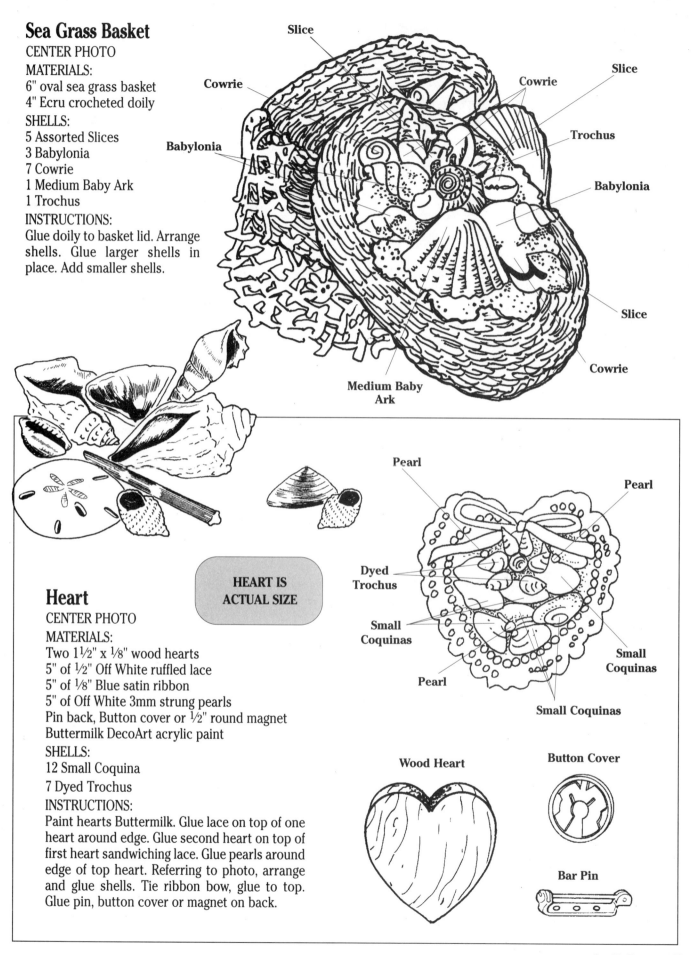

HEART IS ACTUAL SIZE

Heart

CENTER PHOTO

MATERIALS:
Two 1½" x ⅛" wood hearts
5" of ½" Off White ruffled lace
5" of ⅛" Blue satin ribbon
5" of Off White 3mm strung pearls
Pin back, Button cover or ½" round magnet
Buttermilk DecoArt acrylic paint

SHELLS:
12 Small Coquina
7 Dyed Trochus

INSTRUCTIONS:
Paint hearts Buttermilk. Glue lace on top of one heart around edge. Glue second heart on top of first heart sandwiching lace. Glue pearls around edge of top heart. Referring to photo, arrange and glue shells. Tie ribbon bow, glue to top. Glue pin, button cover or magnet on back.

Angel Pin & Earrings

CENTER PHOTO

SHELLS:
Two ¼" Natural wood beads
One ⅜" Natural wood bead
Gold chenille stem
¾" pin back
2 earring posts
DecoArt Crystal Twinkles

SHELLS:
9 Baby Ark, 1 slightly larger (dress)

INSTRUCTIONS:
Place 2 matching arks together on wax paper for wings. Glue ark for dress on top of wings. Glue bead heads. Wrap chenille stem in circles for halos, cut and glue to back of bead. Paint arks with Crystal Twinkles. Allow to dry and remove from wax paper. Glue pin on back of larger angel and ear posts on remaining angels.

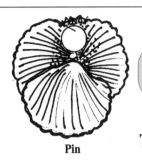

Pin

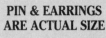

PIN & EARRINGS ARE ACTUAL SIZE

Earrings

To Make Angels:

A. Glue Wings

B. Glue Dress

C. Glue Head and Halo

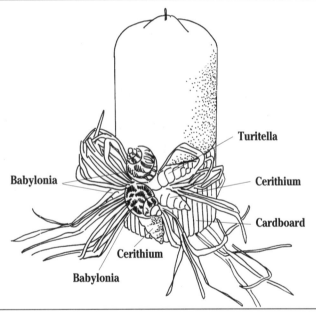

Turitella

Babylonia

Cerithium

Cardboard

Cerithium

Babylonia

Pillar Candle

BACK COVER PHOTO

MATERIALS:
6" pillar candle
3" x 10" of corrugated cardboard
Pinking shears
Raffia

SHELLS:
3 Babylonia   1 Turitella
2 White Cerithium

INSTRUCTIONS:
Cut corrugated cardboard with pinking shears to 2½" wide, wrap around candle and glue in place. Wrap raffia around cardboard, tie in a bow. Glue shells in center of bow.

Cockle

Black Turbo

Black Turbo

Babylonia

Coquina

Mexican Olive

Photo Frame

BACK COVER PHOTO

MATERIALS:
4" x 6" acrylic photo frame

SHELLS:
3 Black Turbo   1 Coquina
1 Babylonia   7 Small Dyed Snail
9 Mexican Olive   1 Cockle
Small piece of coral

INSTRUCTIONS:
Referring to photo, arrange shells and glue to lower corner of frame. Insert your favorite beach photo and display for all to enjoy.

Note: *Photograph taken in 1977 shows my father passing on the family tradition of shell collecting and sand castle building to my 2 year old daughter, Jennie.*

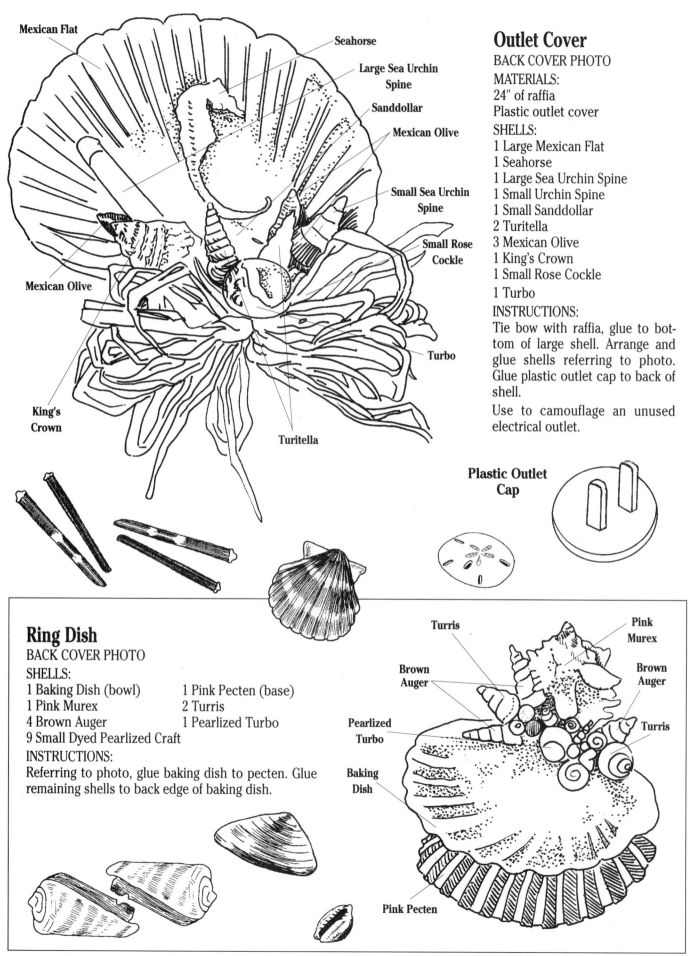

Mexican Flat

Seahorse

Large Sea Urchin Spine

Sanddollar

Mexican Olive

Small Sea Urchin Spine

Small Rose Cockle

Mexican Olive

Turbo

King's Crown

Turitella

Outlet Cover
BACK COVER PHOTO

MATERIALS:
24" of raffia
Plastic outlet cover

SHELLS:
1 Large Mexican Flat
1 Seahorse
1 Large Sea Urchin Spine
1 Small Urchin Spine
1 Small Sanddollar
2 Turitella
3 Mexican Olive
1 King's Crown
1 Small Rose Cockle
1 Turbo

INSTRUCTIONS:
Tie bow with raffia, glue to bottom of large shell. Arrange and glue shells referring to photo. Glue plastic outlet cap to back of shell.

Use to camouflage an unused electrical outlet.

Plastic Outlet Cap

Ring Dish
BACK COVER PHOTO

SHELLS:
1 Baking Dish (bowl)   1 Pink Pecten (base)
1 Pink Murex   2 Turris
4 Brown Auger   1 Pearlized Turbo
9 Small Dyed Pearlized Craft

INSTRUCTIONS:
Referring to photo, glue baking dish to pecten. Glue remaining shells to back edge of baking dish.

Turris

Pink Murex

Brown Auger

Brown Auger

Pearlized Turbo

Turris

Baking Dish

Pink Pecten

Angel Pin

BACK COVER PHOTO

MATERIALS:
1" pin back
½" wood bead
Small piece of Blonde curly hair
Gold ring
¼" Pink porcelain rose
Black fine-tip permanent pen
2 White 4mm x 9mm teardrop pearls

SHELLS:
3 Baby Ark, l slightly larger (dress)
2 Small Snail (hands)

INSTRUCTIONS:
Arrange baby arks flat side down on wax paper. Glue wood bead where shells meet. Glue snail shell on sides of bead and rose and pearls to front. Glue hair to head and Gold ring to shells behind head. Allow to dry, remove from wax paper. Glue pin to back. Dot eyes with pen.

ANGEL PIN IS ACTUAL SIZE

Angel Assembly

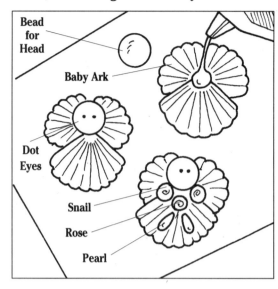

Bead for Head
Baby Ark
Dot Eyes
Snail
Rose
Pearl

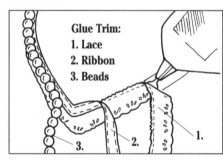

Glue Trim:
1. Lace
2. Ribbon
3. Beads

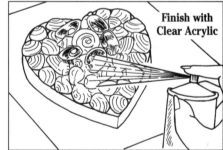

Finish with Clear Acrylic

Heart Box

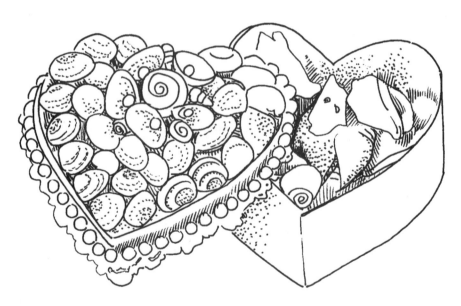

BACK COVER PHOTO

MATERIALS:
3" heart chipwood box
12" of ½" Off White ruffled lace
12" of ⅛" Lavender satin ribbon
12" of White 4mm pearls on a string
Paintbrush
Buttermilk DecoArt acrylic paint

SHELLS:
Small Pink Craft   5 Dove
1 Pearlized Turbo

INSTRUCTIONS:
Paint box Buttermilk. Let dry. Glue lace, ribbon and pearls around edge of lid. Starting at outside edge, arrange and glue craft shells to lid with flat sides down. Glue turbo to top center. Arrange and glue 5 craft shells flat side up around turbo. Referring to photo, glue dove shells between craft shells. Glue a pearl in the 5 craft shells.

A Personal Note About Shells

England has always been a seafaring nation. It has even been said that salt water runs through the veins of the English people! Although the latter may not be true, I must admit that I have always loved the ocean.

Family holidays were always spent at the beach and some of England's best beaches were just two hours away from my home. My parents and I would walk along the beach and collect as many shells as we could find. The shells were then used to decorate a variety of sand castles and cottages, which we'd leave at the end of the day to be swallowed up once more by the incoming tide.

I learned that if you held a shell up to your ear you could hear the ocean tides rushing in and out. I always had shells at home so I could hear the sea, even if I couldn't see it. As an adult, I have yet to walk along a beach without coming back with some kind of shell in my pocket. Shells will always hold an eternal fascination for me and these are some of my favorite projects. I hope you will enjoy them too.

Julie

Shell Directory

Apple Blossom

Baby Ark

Cancellaria
Undulat

Craft

Baking Dish

Babylonia

Coquina

Brown
Auger

Cats' Eye

Dentalium

Bursa Crumena

Mexican
Olive

Cowrie

Coral

Dove

Philippine
Olive

Pecten

King's Crown

Mexican Flat